LOVING , LOSING AND BECOMING

PARESH SINGH RAJPUT

To the ones who have shaped me, supported me, and believed in me- this book belongs to you as much as it does to me.

To **Anupama Singh**, my mother, the heart that made me who I am.

To **Sushanta Kumar Singh**, my father, whose silent strength became my foundation.

To **Sthitiprangya Singh**, my sister, my writing inspiration, and my first critic.

To all my lovely cousins, the ones who made childhood beautiful and life brighter.

To my aunt, whom I lost but never truly lost-because love like hers never fades, it stays, guiding me in ways only the heart can understand.

To my closest friends- Abhi, Hemanta, Akankhya, Dushmant, Jyoti- for standing beside me through every chapter of my life.To my college gang and my office platoon- Abhijit, Astha, Shyam, Tapan, Ashutoshs - for being a part of my journey in ways both big and small.And to my *Lasting Impact, Silent Unfinished* stories for believing that I could be a writer- even when I couldn't see it myself.

Contents

Preface

Love. Loss. Growth. Life often takes us through these phases in ways we never expect- pulling us in with promises, breaking us with goodbyes, and leaving us to piece ourselves back together. Loving, Losing, and Becoming is not just a collection of words; it is a journey. A journey through the rawness of emotions, the ache of regret, the weight of self-doubt, and the quiet strength found in healing.

This book is for those who have felt deeply, who have loved without fear and lost without choice. For the ones who have questioned their worth in the silence of the night, for those who have learned that closure is not given but created. It is for the hearts that have shattered and still found a way to beat again.

There are no perfect endings here, only truths- the kind that remind you that every wound carries wisdom, every goodbye holds a lesson, and every heartbreak is a step toward becoming.

If you have ever loved, lost, and struggled to find yourself again, this book is for you. May these words remind you that your journey is not just about what you've lost, but about everything you are becoming.

With all my heart,
Paresh Singh Rajput

How To Read This Book

*Loving, Losing, and Becoming is not a traditional story.*It is a collection of emotions- woven through poetry, passages, scenes, and conversations. Every piece stands on its own, carrying its own weight, its own meaning. I poured sleepless nights and endless emotions into this, carefully choosing each word to make you feel something real.

This book is divided into phases, each capturing a different part of the journey- from the first spark of love to the quiet acceptance of peace. But there is no fixed path to follow. You can flip to any page, read any piece, and let it speak to you in its own way.

And if these words leave even the smallest mark on you, let me know. Tag me, message me, or share your thoughts on my writing page, **thehighhope** on Instagram. Knowing this book touched even one person makes all those sleepless nights worth it.

Now, go ahead- flip the pages, feel the words, and let the journey begin. I hope it touches your soul.

THE SPARK

Where eyes meet, hearts race, and love whispers its first hello.

Whats Your Type ?

"Bro, what's your type?" his friend asked." Type?" He frowned. "I don't have one. Actually, I find this question so wrong- in fact, the whole concept is wrong."

He leaned forward, frustration clear in his voice. "I'm not buying furniture or a smartphone to look for random features in her.I don't want a checklist, I want a person. A soul. Someone I can give the peace she's been missing in this crowded world. I don't need her to fit into a mold- I want Someone who feels safe enough to be completely herself."

"Love isn't about taking, it's about giving. And I want to give all of mine to her, without expecting anything in return. You get it? "

His friend stared at him for a second, then sighed.
"Yeah, I got it... but I was actually asking about the charger."

The First Spark

The first day of college- new place, new faces, new
beginnings. He parked his bike, taking in the chaos
around him. The campus buzzed with excitement, a sea of
fresh starts just like his.

And then, he saw her.
One face, in a crowd of many, yet somehow... different.

Why did she stand out?
Why did her eyes feel like poetry?
Why was her smile so effortlessly calming?
Why did the sunlight seem to dance in her hair?

For a moment, everything else faded.
She was beautiful.

And he was already lost.

He Stayed Still

She was a storm- loud, bright, impossible to ignore.
He was the quiet sky before the rain

She was a crashing wave- restless, free, refusing to stay.
He was the lighthouse- silent, steady, standing still.

She spoke, and the room listened.
He watched, and no one noticed.

She thrived in chaos, danced with the noise.
He belonged to the quiet, lost in his own world.

Yet, in a crowd full of faces, she caught herself staring at one
because in a world that never stopped moving-
He stayed still.

What Attracts ?

"What attracts the most? Face? Personality?" someone asked.
"Maybe even salary?" another added with a smirk.

She smiled, shaking her head.

"Effort," she replied. "The way someone chooses you- not just once, but every day. The way they listen, not just to respond, but to understand. The way they make you feel seen, even in a crowded room. Looks fade, charm wears off, money comes and goes... but effort? Effort is love in action. And that's what truly lasts."

She hadn't even finished her sentence yet-
and somewhere in that room, a guy had already fallen for her.

He would Never Forget

She asked him, "**Can you drop me? It's raining, and I can't find an Uber.**"
His heart skipped a beat. **This....this exact moment- was something he had wished for ages.**

As she got into the car, the world outside blurred into a symphony of raindrops, but inside, there was silence. Not the awkward kind, but the kind that feels like a secret only they understand. The conversation faded, replaced by stolen glances and unspoken words.

He wished this drive would never end.

Her wet hair clung to her face, and a single raindrop traced its way down her cheek, making her look even more breathtaking. She, too, felt something- an unfamiliar kind of safety, a warmth that had nothing to do with the car's heater.

They reached her destination, but the rain hadn't stopped. Neither of them moved. He turned on the radio to fill the silence, and as if the universe had conspired for this moment, the first notes of a timeless song played-

"Abhi na jao chhod kar... dil abhi bhara nahi."

He nearly laughed. Thank you, God.

But when he stole a glance at her, she seemed unfazed, lost in her own thoughts. Maybe the song didn't mean anything to her. Maybe this moment was his alone.

Finally, the rain eased, and she picked up her things to leave. Just as she stepped out, she turned back and, with the softest smile, said-

"Abhi nahi jaungi toh kal kaise milenge phir?"

His mind froze. Wait... what? What did she just say?

She stole another smile and walked away, leaving him sitting there, replaying her words over and over.

And just like that, the night became one he would never forget.

The Crush Effect

Having a crush is like signing up for emotional chaos without even realizing it.

Suddenly, everything changes. The way she dresses, the way she fixes her hair, even the way she laughs-
she becomes hyper-aware of it all. She starts checking her phone a little too often, hoping for a notification that might not even come. If he's around, her heart beats faster, but she'll act like she didn't even notice him... except she definitely did.

Every little thing he does feels significant. The way he remembers a random detail about her, the way he laughs, the way his eyes light up when he talks about something he loves- suddenly, she's noticing everything. One text from him can turn her entire bad day around, and one dry reply can make her overthink for hours.

Then there's the teasing from friends. They don't let her breathe when he's around. The nudges, the side-eyes, the whispered "There he is!"- it's game over. She tries to act normal, but the blush creeping onto her face betrays her every single time.

And yet, despite all the nervousness, the awkward moments, and the overthinking, having a crush is kind of magical. It's that feeling of excitement, of butterflies, of hoping- of feeling something real in a world that often feels too predictable.

She knows I exist ?

She accepted his request.
For a second, he just stared at the screen, his heart racing. "Was it real? Did she actually see my name and choose to accept it?"

A stupid smile crept onto his face. She knows he exists now. It was just a small thing- a tap on her screen. But to him? It was everything.

Suddenly, a million thoughts rushed through his mind. *"Should I text her? Should I wait? What if she doesn't reply? What if she does? "*

He took a deep breath, his fingers hovering over the keyboard.
One step closer. And for now, that was enough.

The Office Crush

She didn't see it coming.
At first, he was just the new joinee- the one who fumbled with the office coffee machine, who took a little too long to understand the never-ending email chains, and who always greeted everyone with an awkward yet endearing smile.

He was clumsy, always misplacing his ID card, accidentally hitting 'Reply All' on emails, and panicking over small mistakes like a nervous intern.

But then, she started noticing things.

The way he adjusted his tie before an important meeting, the way he scribbled notes furiously during team huddles, the way his face lit up when he finally got something right. There was something so effortlessly innocent and eager about him- like he was still discovering the world, one Excel sheet at a time.

Her friends noticed before she did.

"You've been awfully interested in onboarding lately," one teased over lunch.
"Are you sure you're mentoring him or secretly crushing on him?" another smirked.

She scoffed, brushing it off , "**He is younger... It's so silly guys**". But she couldn't help it- every time someone brought him up, she felt the heat rise to her cheeks.

And then, one day, he walked past, flashing her that effortless, cluelessly charming smile, and her heart skipped a beat.

Maybe- just maybe- it wasn't that silly after all.

Something Changed !

That day, something changed.
She had always been his friend- the one who stole his fries, who laughed at his terrible jokes, who never needed to try too hard to be beautiful.

But that evening, when she walked in wearing a deep red saree draped perfectly around her, with delicate golden borders catching the light, he couldn't look away. The small bindi was resting perfectly on her forehead ... like a quiet statement, her jhumkas swayed with every little movement with every step, and when she tucked a loose strand of hair behind her ear, he felt his heart skip a beat .

Her kohl-lined eyes held a spark, the kind that made everything else blur. The bangles on her wrists jingled softly as she fixed the pleats of her saree, unaware of the way his heart had begun to race. She wasn't just his friend anymore- not in that moment.

He was looking at someone he wanted to know all over again.For the first time, he realized- this was more than just familiarity, more than just friendship. This was something new, something unknown. And for the first time, he let himself feel it.

Felt Different

They had always been just colleagues- friends, at most. A constant presence in each other's daily chaos, sharing coffee breaks, rolling eyes at meetings, arguing over the last slice of pizza. It was effortless, light.

But that evening, something shifted.

As they walked out of the office, he stretched, looked at her, and said, "Alright then, bye."
Just bye ? No teasing ? , no "See yaa, dumbo!" ? like he always said.

She paused. Why did it feel... off? She had heard this word from him a hundred times before, yet today, it sounded different. Felt different.

As he walked away, she found herself watching- really watching. The way he ran his fingers through his hair, how his shoulders relaxed as he hummed some random tune.

And just like that, a thought slipped in, uninvited but undeniable- Why does this feel like something more
She smiled to herself. Maybe it was nothing.

Or maybe, it was the beginning of something she wasn't ready to name yet.

The Beauty of having a Crush

"She's in a relationship, man." what they say .

Okay, and? If I like her, what's her fault in that? They say it like I'm expecting something in return, like every feeling needs to be a two-way street. But that's the thing- they don't get it.

Liking someone isn't about owning them. It's not about making a move or expecting a happy ending. Sometimes, it's just about looking at someone and feeling lighter, about watching them laugh and thinking, yeah, that's enough.

I don't need to talk to her. I don't need her to like me back. I don't even need her to know. Because that's the best part about having a crush?

It's just... pure. No expectations, no demands- just a quiet kind of happiness that exists simply because she does. And honestly, what's wrong with that?

15

"What is a crush?" they ask.
"Just an illusion," I say. "Once you truly know them, the magic fades or love begins."

CHAPTER TWO

THE FALL

When feelings grow, unspoken words ache, and love demands to be known.

Love

Love isn't in the way they look,
Or how they turn heads when they walk.

It's not in the smile that fades so quick,
Or the words that slip through a charming talk.

Love isn't in the way they dress,
Or the compliments they say to impress.

It's not in the way they catch your eye,
Or the way they make your heart race high.

Love is in the quiet moments shared,
In the way they listen, the way they care.
It's in the small things they do every day,
That show they want to stay.

Love is in the little things they do,
Like remembering your favorite food.
It's in the texts when you're feeling down,
Or when they smile without a frown.

It's not about looks, it's about the vibe,
The way they make you feel alive.

It's not about the attraction you see,
It's about the person who sets your soul free.

The Confession

The last day of school. She watched him from afar, hugging his friends, giving farewell embraces. Yes, they hadn't talked much, but their eyes had spoken a language of their own.

They never laughed together, yet their presence brought each other peace.They never confessed, yet there was a quiet, unspoken possessiveness between them.

And now, a dark cloud was about to settle over her heart as she realized- this might be the last time she'd see him. But before the weight of goodbye could sink in, a voice called from behind.

A voice she knew. A voice her heart had memorized.

Her heartbeat quickened, time stood still-
And in the middle of all the farewells,

the confession happened.

Felt Like Home

He came home late, exhaustion weighing on his shoulders. The city still felt unfamiliar... new streets, new faces, nothing that truly felt like home.

As he dropped his bag on the couch, his phone buzzed. A message popped up on the screen.

"Ordered your favorite food, it's on the way. Please pick it up. And you're welcome... Oh, and I love you too."

A tired sigh turned into a smile. In the middle of all the chaos, there she was- his piece of comfort, his quiet warmth.And in that moment, he realized how lucky he was.

Love wasn't just in words; it was in the little ways she made him feel at home, no matter where he was.

She had the Best

Her friends kept telling her she deserved better-

that he didn't give her enough time, that love should be louder, grander.

But how could she explain the way he knew her in ways no one else did?

How he remembered her favorite café and ordered her usual without asking.
How he sent her ice cream on bad days, knowing exactly what flavor she needed.
How his phone had a note filled with her favorite things- songs, movies, little dreams she once mentioned in passing.
How he reminded her to carry an umbrella before she even saw the clouds.
How he never forgot the dates that even she overlooked- her exam, her big meeting, the day she lost someone she loved.
How he even knew when her period was coming, sending her chocolates before the cramps kicked in and checking in with a simple "Take some rest, baby."

And then there were his messages-
"Have you eaten?"
"Did you reach home safe?"
"Is something bothering you? I'm listening, baby."
"Why does your smile look faded today? I hate it."

It wasn't just words. It was the way he noticed, even when

she tried to hide it.

The way he understood, even when she had no words to say.The way he loved- not loudly, but deeply.
And in those little things, she found more than enough reason to stay.

Because she already had the best.

Men In Love

Men in love are the cutest.
They say, "I don't care," then drop a message- "Have you eaten?"
They roll their eyes at drama but remember the little things- how you like your coffee, the way your voice changes when you're tired.
They act unbothered, yet their jacket somehow ends up around your shoulders when it's cold.
They won't always say the right words, but they'll show up, stay late, and make sure you're safe.
Because love, for them, isn't about grand gestures.

It's in the small, quiet moments-
in the way they stay, even when they don't say.

She Fell for Him Again

It was another family gathering, and the conversation started to take a turn. Everyone was talking about how she should focus more on home now that she was married. She felt her chest tighten, the pressure building with every word. She tried to speak up, but it was like her voice wasn't enough.Her heart sank as the conversation grew louder, and for a moment, she wished she could disappear.

But then, she felt his hand gently brush against hers. She turned to look at him, and there was a calm determination in his eyes. He stood up, clearing his throat, and in that moment, everything seemed to stop.

"I don't think it's fair to ask her to choose," he said, his voice steady, unwavering. "She's worked hard for this, and if she wants to continue, then that's her choice. I support her, and I will always support her, no matter what.

Everyone went quiet. It wasn't what they expected, and it definitely wasn't what she expected.

She turned to him, eyes wide. "You're okay with it?"

He just smiled. "Of course. I want you to do what makes you happy. You don't have to choose between your dreams and being a wife."

The room fell silent. His words hung in the air, a shield around her. She was speechless, not from surprise, but from the sheer strength he had shown in defending her. His support wasn't just a fleeting gesture- it was genuine, a promise he didn't need to make with words. He was standing by her, giving her the space to be herself, to chase her dreams without feeling guilty.

As she looked at him, something shifted inside her. For the first time, she saw him not just as her husband, but as the man who would always have her back. The man who believed in her even when she doubted herself.

And in that moment, she realized- she had fallen in love with him... again. Not because of what he had done for her, but because of the way he made her feel: valued, respected, and truly seen.

We Made It

"They won't last."
"It's just a phase."
"They'll grow out of it."

That's what everyone said when we chose each other . They doubted us, whispered that real relationships needed more than just a spark.

But love isn't about proving people wrong; it's about proving each other right.

We had our fights, our silent treatments, our "maybe this isn't working" moments. But we always found our way back. Not because it was easy, but because it was worth it.

We learned that love isn't just about grand gestures- it's in the patience when one is upset, in the effort to understand rather than just respond, in the choice to stay when walking away seemed easier.

Half the battle was already won the moment we decided never to give up on each other. And today, as our wedding invitations land in the hands of those who doubted us, we don't say, "We proved you wrong."

We simply say, "We made it."

The Old Love

They were no longer young, the years had marked their faces with gentle lines and silver strands in their hair. But when he saw her again, across the room, it felt like the world stood still for just a moment. Time had been kind to her, like a soft breeze carrying the scent of memories. She was still beautiful, her smile still held the same warmth that had once made his heart race.

They never married, never lived the life they had once imagined together. But as he stood there, watching her, he realized that some loves are not meant to last forever-they're meant to be remembered, cherished, and admired from a far.

Love, he thought, is not always about achieving the dream, sometimes it's about appreciating the beauty of an incomplete wish.

The love they had wasn't perfect, it wasn't the fairytale they had hoped for, but it was real. And in that moment, he knew that sometimes, the most beautiful love stories are the ones that are never fully written, but always felt deeply in the heart.

The Option Game

Love isn't a game of options.

In a world where everything is replaceable- phones, jobs, even people- we've started treating love the same way. If something feels difficult, if someone doesn't meet our expectations instantly, we tell ourselves, there are plenty of options. Swipe left, move on, find someone new.

But is that love?

Love isn't about finding the next best thing. It's about choosing the same person, over and over, even when it's not easy. Because if you keep searching for someone better, you'll always find them- there will always be someone funnier, more attractive, more exciting- someone who, at first glance, seems like an upgrade.But what happens when you realize that better doesn't mean deeper? That new doesn't mean real? Love isn't about upgrades.

It's not about walking away the moment things feel uncertain or imperfect. Because love will get hard. The spark will dim, comfort will replace excitement, and there will be days when choosing them doesn't feel effortless. But that's when love begins- not when it ends.It's about choice. About looking at the same person, day after day, argument after argument, and still choosing them. Not because they're perfect, but because what you have is real. Because you know that love isn't about who makes your heart race for a moment, but who stays when life slows down.

Because at the end of the day, what stays isn't the thrill of something new- it's the depth of something real.

The Illusion of Love at First Sight

When you choose someone just because they caught your eye- because they smiled a certain way, carried themselves with confidence, or had a voice that made your heart skip- you're not choosing them. You're choosing a version of them, a reflection of what you want to see.

But love? Love isn't just admiration. It's not just the charm, the laughter, or the moments that shine. It's the quiet battles, the unspoken fears, the past they don't bring up in conversations.

When you love someone, you don't just get their best- you get their worst. Their insecurities, their scars, the parts of themselves they're still learning to accept.

That's why love at first sight is a myth. Because love isn't just about seeing someone. It's about staying even after you've seen it all.

What is Love ?

So, Love... What Is It?

Is it a grand proposal under the stars? A dreamy destination wedding with picture- perfect vows? No? Maybe a long caption on social media, flexing a love that looks flawless?Or is it showing the world how lucky you are to have them?

Maybe. But love isn't just what the world sees.

Love is not measured in grand gestures; it hides in the quiet moments.

It's the way they pull the blanket over you when you fall asleep on the couch.
It's how they send you a "Did you eat?" text on a hectic day.
It's the way they remember the little things- how you hate the sound of balloons popping or how you rewatch the same movie when you're sad.

It's how their voice sounds like home after a long day.
It's trust that doesn't need constant reassurance.
It's respect that doesn't waver, even in arguments
It's choosing each other- on good days, bad days, and the days in between.

Love isn't always fireworks. Sometimes, it's just a hand reaching out in the dark, a presence that says, "I'm here. I'm staying."

Because love? It's not just a feeling. It's a choice. Every single day.

CHAPTER THREE

THE DRIFT

When change creeps in. Conversations fade, distances form, and what once felt close now feels unfamiliar-sometimes with people, sometimes within ourselves.

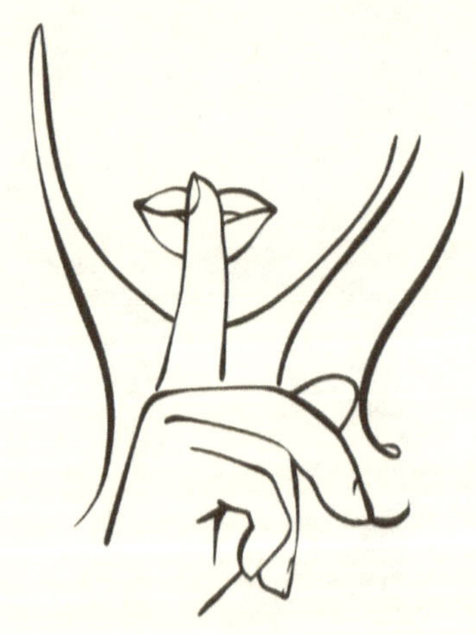

Is That Too Much to Ask ?

She never asked for much.
She never demanded grand gestures, never expected long love letters .

All she ever wanted were the little things- the effort, the understanding, the warmth of knowing she mattered.

"Is it really that hard to listen when I speak?" she asked, her voice softer than she intended."Is it too much to expect you to notice when I'm upset?"

She wasn't asking for the moon. Just for him to look at her- really look at her- when she spoke. To hold her hand when she was anxious. To reassure her when her mind spiraled into overthinking. To care, not out of obligation, but because he wanted to.

"They say women want too much," she scoffed bitterly. "But all I ever wanted was for you to care the way I cared for you."

She wasn't asking for love she had to beg for. She was asking for the bare minimum- and even that, it seemed, was too much.

The Overlooked Pain

She sighs a little louder,
hoping he'll ask,
but he doesn't.

He stays quiet longer,
hoping she'll notice,
but she doesn't.

She turns away in bed.
He scrolls through his phone.
Two hearts inches apart,
but miles away.

Once, they used to ask,
"What's wrong?"
"Are you okay?"
Now, they assume-
"She'll be fine."
"He doesn't want to talk."

When did love turn into silence?
When did we stop being
each other's safe place?

The Presence

The Presence That Feels Like Absence .
They sit together, just like they used to. Same couch, same room, same routine. But something is missing.

One is glued to their phone, scrolling through endless notifications, replying to messages, laughing at something on the screen. The other? Watching them- waiting, hoping.

Hoping they'd look up.
Hoping they'd notice the silence between them.
Hoping they'd remember how they used to talk for hours, how their presence once felt like home.

But now, they feel like background noise in their own relationship. Like a song that once played on repeat but now just fades into the distance.

They're still here, together.
But somehow, it feels lonelier than being alone.

You Told Me..

You told me you loved me the way I am,
then why did you make fun of my insecurities?
Why did you laugh at the things I hid,
the scars I never wanted to show?

You said my fears were safe with you,
then why did you use them to break me?
Why did your words feel like knives,
cutting exactly where it hurt the most?

You promised I was enough,
then why did I feel so small with you?
Why did I have to shrink myself,
just to fit inside your love?

Something Couldn't Fix ...

They sat across from each other, a table between them, but the real distance was far greater.

"You don't get it, do you?" he said, his voice quiet but firm. "It's not about jealousy. It's about boundaries."

She sighed, crossing her arms. "I treat everyone the same. I don't see why that's a problem."

"That's exactly the problem," he said, leaning forward. "If I'm just another person in your life, if the way you talk to me, the way you make space for me, is the same as everyone else- then what's the point ?"

She shifted in her seat, avoiding his eyes. "You're overthinking this."

"No," he said. "I just finally see it for what it is."

Her fingers tightened around the edge of the table. "So... what? You want me to change who I am?"
He sighed, a kind of tired that went beyond just this conversation.

"I just realized that I don't want to be in a place where I have to beg to be treated like I matter more. I just want to be with someone who knows the difference between being kind to everyone and making someone feel irreplaceable."

And in that silence, he understood- this wasn't something

they could fix.He stood up, sliding his chair back slowly. "We're done, aren't we?"

She had no answer.And just like that, it was over.

The One-Sided Effort

I text first.
I call first.
I plan, I wait, I hope.

You reply when you feel like it.
You show up when it's convenient.
You never ask, "How was your day?"
But I still ask about yours.

I made excuses for you-
"Maybe they're busy."
"Maybe they're tired."
"Maybe they don't realize."

But then one day, I stopped.
Stopped texting.
Stopped calling.
Stopped trying.

And you?
You didn't even notice.

The Attention

The Attention That's No Longer Yours .

There was a time when your name popping up on their screen meant everything. You could almost hear the excitement in their voice when they picked up your call. Their replies came instantly, sometimes even before you finished typing. They used to share everything- their random thoughts, their late-night cravings, the funny things they saw on the way to work.

But now... now it's different.

Now, you double-text and stare at the screen, waiting for a reply that comes hours later, sometimes not at all. Their laughter, once reserved for you, now rings louder for someone else. They used to share their day with you before anyone else- now, you see it in their stories, posted for the world to see.

You tell yourself it's nothing. People get busy, right? But deep down, you know. It's not that they stopped loving you. It's just that they stopped loving you first. And maybe, just maybe, they've started loving someone else instead.

The Excuses

"I'm just tired."
"You know how I am."
"Work has been crazy lately."
"It's not a big deal, you're overreacting."
"Why do we have to talk about this again?"

But the calls became shorter.
The good mornings stopped.
The effort faded.
The little things that once mattered don't exist anymore.

Nothing has changed, they say.
But you can feel it-
Everything has.

You Were My Home

You used to text first,
now I wait for a reply that never comes.

You used to hold my hand like you'd never let go,
now you don't even notice when I pull away.

Your "I love you" once felt like a promise,
now it feels like something you just say.

You made me feel special,
now I feel like just another routine.

I wonder when the shift happened-
when my laughter stopped being your favorite sound,

Love didn't end all at once-
it faded in forgotten texts, dry conversations,
and the way you stopped looking at me like you used to.

The spark that once lit up my world,
now flickers like a dying flame.

Funny how someone who was once my home,
now feels like a place I'm no longer welcome in.

They Both Did

They stood across from each other in the courtroom for divorce, the silence between them louder than any argument they ever had. Papers were signed, decisions made, yet their eyes met- searching, speaking without words.

"We promised we wouldn't give up."
"May be...One of us was lying."

His fingers twitched, remembering the warmth of her hand. Her breath hitched, recalling the way he used to say her name. But love wasn't about who held on the longest- it was about who let go first.

And today, they both did

CHAPTER FOUR

THE SHATTER

The breaking point. The unexpected goodbye, the quiet exit, the moment when something you held onto slips away- love, trust, a dream, or even a version of yourself.

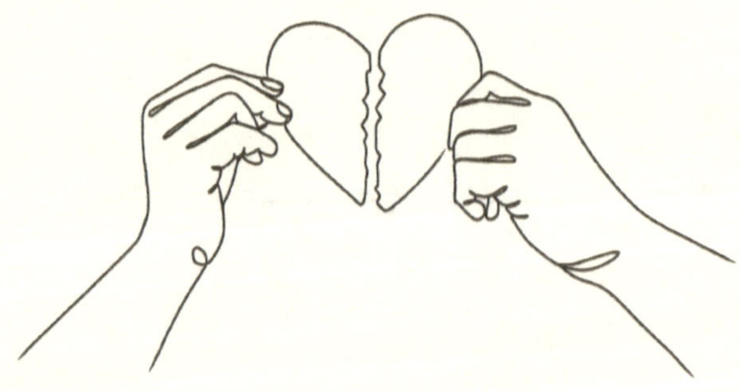

Never Got Closure

One day, it was laughter, late-night calls, and "take care" texts. The next? Silence. No fight, no warning- just distance where warmth used to be.

At first, you told yourself they were busy. That they'd come back. That maybe something happened. But then, days turned into weeks. Weeks into months. And the realization settled in like a weight on your chest- they were never coming back.

You replay the last conversation, looking for signs you might have missed. Were they already halfway out the door while you were still making plans? Did they know it was the last time they'd say your name, yet said nothing?

You draft messages you never send. "Did I do something wrong?" "Can we talk?" "I just need to understand." But deep down, you know- if they wanted to explain, they would have.

And so, you're left with nothing but questions. Questions like , "Did I not deserve a proper goodbye?"

No closure. No final words.
Just the echoes of a love that disappeared without a goodbye.

Once I begged for Love

I loved with open hands,
but you held me with crossed fingers.

I stayed when you wavered,
waited while you wandered,
trusted when I shouldn't have.

You whispered forever,
but meant for now.
You held my heart,
but never with care

And I?
I kept breaking just to keep you whole.

But love should never feel like begging.
And I should have never had to ask to be chosen.

Her Breath belong to Him

The folded flag sat neatly on the table, untouched, unmoved- just like her. The uniform still smelled like him, hanging in the closet as if he would step into it any second now. His boots, still by the door. His voice, still echoing in the walls.

Everyone told her she was strong. That she should be proud. That he died a hero. But what they didn't understand was- he was her home, and now, she was homeless.

Nights were the hardest. She still set the table for two, still turned to his side of the bed, only to be met with cold sheets. Sometimes, she swore she heard his laughter. Sometimes, she whispered his name into the silence, hoping the wind would carry it to wherever he was.

She had memorized the weight of his absence. And yet, she couldn't bring herself to believe he was truly gone.

Because how could he be, when every breath she took still belonged to him?

Who Told You?

"Who told you to love her?" they say,
"Who made you hope she would stay?"

No one. She never asked me to fall,
Never promised me anything at all.

"Who told you to wait, to believe?"
"To chase a dream that she'd never weave?"

No one. It was just me and my heart,
Building a hope where love wouldn't start.

"Who told you to break, to bend?"
"To hold on tight when she saw the end?"

I built a home in a heart that was never mine,
Watered the roots, but it gave me no sign.

But love doesn't ask what's right,
It just burns... and I let it ignite.

You Lost Yourself

The Betrayal That Changed Everything .
It wasn't just that they left- it was how they left. The way they looked you in the eye and made promises they never intended to keep. The way they held your hand like it meant something, even when their heart had already wandered.

Maybe they swore forever but disappeared overnight, leaving nothing but unanswered calls and a hollow silence. Maybe you weren't the only one, even though their lips said you were. The betrayal wasn't just in their actions- it was in the lies they made sound like love.

At first, you thought heartbreak was about losing someone. But then, you realized it was also about losing trust. About questioning every I love you that once made you smile. About doubting if love itself is even real or just another beautifully wrapped deception.

And the worst part? It wasn't just them you lost.
You lost the version of yourself who believed in them.

"Who asked you to do ?" they said.
I smiled.... because that was the moment I shattered.

~Random

Never Saw that Coming

She trusted him- blindly, completely .

She believed in his late replies, his half-hearted apologies, the way he held her close yet still felt miles away. She ignored the signs, convinced herself that love meant patience, that doubt was just insecurity in disguise.

"You're overthinking."
"You know you're the only one."
"I would never hurt you."

She wanted to believe him. So she did. Until the truth ripped through her like a blade she never saw coming. A name she didn't recognize. A conversation she was never meant to read. A version of him she didn't know existed.

It wasn't just that he cheated. It was how easily he lied. How effortlessly he lived two lives- one with her, built on promises, and another, hidden in the shadows of secrecy.

She replayed every moment in her head, trying to find the exact second when love turned into betrayal. When trust became blindness. When she became just another person who gave her heart to someone who never deserved it.

And the worst part? He didn't even seem sorry. Because for him, it was just a mistake. But for her, it was the moment everything shattered.

I trusted someone with all my heart, without a second thought,
without a reason- just pure, blind faith.
And they gave me a reason, a lesson,

a scar that whispers, "Never again."

~Random

Sometimes ...Love isn't Enough

They tried. God knows they tried.

Through every whispered doubt, every warning disguised as advice, every late-night conversation filled with fragile hope-

"We'll figure it out."
"We just need time."
"Love wins, right?"

But love doesn't break traditions. Love doesn't rewrite family names or erase the weight of expectations.

The hall was filled with people, laughter, and the echoes of wedding rituals passed down for generations. She sat there, draped in red and gold, her hands adorned with henna that traced a story different from the one she had dreamed of. The weight of jewelry on her skin was nothing compared to the weight in her chest.

Somewhere in the crowd, he stood- unseen, unwanted. His fists clenched, nails digging into his palm, but no pain could compare to the one twisting inside him. He wanted to scream, to run to her, to remind her of the life they had dreamed of. But tonight, words had no place. Only silence.

She didn't stop loving him. She just couldn't fight anymore. And when the day came, she walked down the aisle- not towards him, but towards the life she was told to choose. He wasn't there to stop it. He wasn't even allowed to try.

The priest's voice rang through the air. Promises made. Vows spoken. Fire crackling as they walked in circles- each step pulling her further away from him.

She didn't look for him. She couldn't. Because if she did, if their eyes met, she knew she'd break. And tonight, there was no room for breaking. Only for obeying.

And he just stood there, watching. Knowing that no matter how hard they had fought, love had lost. Because sometimes, love isn't about holding on. Sometimes, it's about watching the person you would have chosen in every lifetime walk away- because in this one, they just couldn't stay.

THE HAUNTING

The echoes of what was. The memories that refuse to fade, the "almosts" that still sting, the people and moments that linger in the quiet corners of your mind.

Heart Skipped a Beat

He thought he had moved on. Thought time had done its job, sealing away the past where it belonged.
But then, one day, he saw someone like her- sitting on the front seat.

The way she tucked her hair behind her ear, the way she glanced at her phone. For a second, his heart skipped a beat.His hands went cold, his chest felt heavy. It was just a glimpse, just a stranger. But in that moment, it felt like everything rewound.

And that's when he realized- maybe he never really moved on. He just learned how to live with it.

She's not Her Anymore

She's forgetting to smile at her own reflection.
Forgetting to hum her favorite song while tying her hair.

Her bookshelf stands untouched, the stories she once loved
now just silent pages.
Her skincare bottles remain unopened- she no longer cares
if her skin glows.
The stray dogs she used to wave at still look for her, but she
walks past them, lost in thoughts.
She doesn't click pictures of sunsets anymore.
Doesn't try on different earrings just for fun.
Doesn't send long voice notes rambling about nothing.
Her favorite lip tint is drying up, untouched.
Her Pinterest boards of cute outfits and dream vacations
stay the same- no new pins, no new dreams.

No late-night cravings for chocolate. No random texts filled
with heart emojis.
She doesn't dance around in oversized t-shirts, doesn't
giggle at silly memes, doesn't blush at love songs.

She's still here, but she's not her anymore.

Not on the Menu

In the middle of his drink, the waiter came,
"Would you like to order, sir?"- the same old name.

He looked up, eyes lost in the past,
A heart once whole, now breaking fast.

"Do you have anything that feels like home?"
"Because I lost mine in her," he spoke alone.

But love was never a choice to buy,
Not something served, no matter the cry.

Drunk enough to say it out loud,
Sober enough to know- love's not allowed.

She Moved On

She Moved On, He Stayed Behind .

She let go so effortlessly, like the love they built was just a phase, a fleeting moment she had already prepared to leave. He, on the other hand, stayed stuck- replaying conversations, overanalyzing the silence she left behind.

She found someone new before the dust had even settled. Maybe she had a backup plan, a soft place to land before she even walked away. Or maybe, for her, moving on was just easier.

He wonders if she ever really meant it- the promises, the late-night confessions, the way she once looked at him like he was everything. Now, she looks at someone else that way, and he's left questioning if he was ever more than just a temporary stop on her way to something better.

She moved on. He still lingers. And somehow, that hurts more .

Cause of Death

"The doctor said... we can't write that down,
it's illogical, doesn't make sense."

But how do I explain the silence inside me?
The way my heart stopped in past tense?

No wounds, no blood, no final breath,
just a slow unraveling, a quiet death.

"Cause of death?" they ask again-
Seeing her with someone else.

Addicted to Her

He didn't realize when it happened. When her habits became his, when her world blended into his own. He used to roll his eyes at her obsession with chai at odd hours, but now, every evening, he finds himself making a cup, only to leave it untouched. He never understood why she always hummed the same old song under her breath- until he caught himself doing it absentmindedly in the middle of a meeting.

The places she loved now feel empty without her. The bookstore where she'd lose track of time, the café where she'd steal bites from his plate even after saying she wasn't hungry. The little things he once found annoying- the way she corrected his grammar, the way she left voice notes instead of texting- he misses them the most.

And the worst part? He's started using her phrases.

"*Am just a baby,*" he sighed the other day, the exact way she used to. His friend raised an eyebrow, confused at his sudden change in vocabulary.

He thought he'd move on, thought time would make it easier. But she's everywhere. In the words he speaks, in the spaces she filled, in the silence she left behind. He was never one to believe in ghosts, but now, he carries one inside him- haunting, lingering, refusing to let go.

Never truly yours

He had said, "I don't like being ignored." Yet, in the end, she made silence their only language.
He had said, "I don't like goodbyes." But she left without turning back, as if he was just another stop along the way.
He had said, "I don't like broken promises." Still, she made him believe in forever, only to teach him that some forevers come with an expiration date.

And once, in a moment that felt like love, she had said, "I love your eyes."
Now, those same eyes ache from searching for something that was never his to keep.

He never thought healing would mean unlearning her- rewriting every moment, every word, every touch.
Yet here he is, taking longer to forget her than the time he even knew her.

Because heartbreak isn't just about losing someone- it's about realizing they were never truly yours to begin with.

The Goodbye She Never Wanted

She always hated saying "bye"- it felt too cold, too final. So she made him say "tata" instead, a silly little habit that became theirs.

Now, he has to say "goodbye" for real. And she misses the person she lost, knowing it was her fault.

How Could They?

How could they hold my hand like it was meant to be there forever- only to let go like it was nothing?
How could they look at me like I was the only thing that mattered- only to turn away like I never did?

How could they make me believe I was special, irreplaceable, theirs- only to prove I was just another name they'd one day forget?
If there was nothing in their heart, why did they make mine race?
If they never planned to stay, why did they make me feel like home?
If it was all just a moment to them, why does it feel like a lifetime to me?

How do people do that
How do they give you everything- only to walk away as if it was never real?

Everything to Nothing

They're still here- posting, laughing, living. Their world didn't stop, not even for a second. But somewhere along the way, you stopped being a part of it. No more late-night check-ins, no more inside jokes that only the two of you understood. One day, they were yours, and the next, they were someone else's late-night call, someone else's "good morning" text.

You used to be their favorite person. Now, you're just someone they used to know. And the worst part? They don't even seem to notice the difference.

How do you go from being everything to being nothing at all?

CHAPTER SIX

THE REGRET

The weight of 'what ifs.' The unsaid words, the missed chances, the self-doubt , the love not fought for, the time wasted on things that no longer matter.

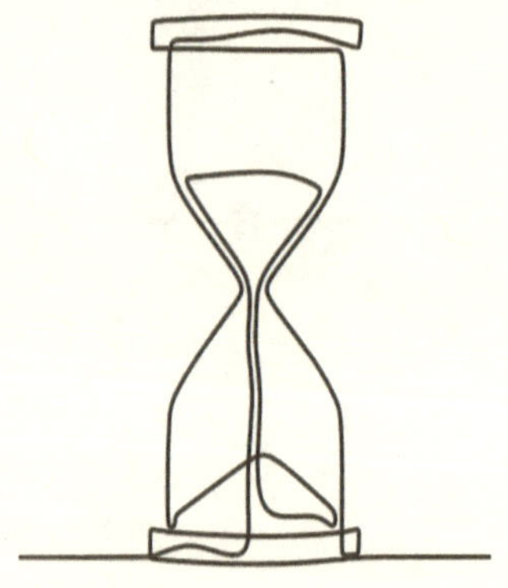

Ache of Self-doubt

Was my presence really too much for them?
Did I speak when I should've stayed silent?
Was I too available, too kind, too open?
Did I overdo the love, or did I just offer it to the wrong
person?

They never said I was wrong,
but they never made me feel right either.

I kept shrinking myself,
thinking maybe if I took up less space,
they would finally want me to stay.

Maybe I wasn't exciting enough.
Maybe I wasn't quiet enough.
Maybe I wasn't soft enough.
Maybe I just wasn't enough.

Every overthought message,
every second-guess of my own worth,
was me trying to fit into a space
that was never meant to hold me.

And now I'm left wondering-
Was I really that unbearable to love?
Or did they just never try?

What if...

What if I stayed a little longer?
What if I fought a little harder?

What if I said the words I hid?
Would it have changed the way we lived?

What if I reached instead of ran?
What if I held on to your hand?

What if love was just a choice?
And I had dared to raise my voice?

But "what ifs" are a cruel game,
Yet I still whisper them.... your name.

A Letter That Was Never Sent

"Hey... I don't even know why I'm writing this. Maybe because I still have things to say. Maybe because I still hope you'd listen. I don't know.

I hope you're doing well. I wanted to say I'm sorry- for the things I said, for the things I didn't. For not understanding when I should have, for holding on when I should have let go.

I wanted to tell you I loved you. That I still do, maybe in a different way. Maybe in a way that no longer asks for anything in return. But what's the point now?

Take care. "

And that day, like all the others before it, she couldn't bring herself to hit send.

May be I wasn't . . .

Maybe I was not good enough.

Maybe no matter how much I cared,
how much I tried,
how much I stayed-
it was never going to be me.

Maybe I was just a place for her to rest,
not the home she wanted to stay in.

Maybe I was the hand she held in the dark,
but not the light she was looking for.

Maybe I was just a lesson she had to learn,
while she was the love I wanted to keep.

Maybe I was the right person at the wrong time,
or maybe, I was never right at all.

And maybe, that's what hurts the most.

Its Cutting me Inside

The regret is cutting me in places I didn't know could bleed.

We met by accident- two souls colliding in a moment neither of us saw coming. It wasn't planned, it wasn't forced; it just was. And for a while, that was enough.

But we didn't lose each other to time or distance. We weren't torn apart by fate. No, we separated by choice- your choice. Or maybe mine. Or maybe both of us, too stubborn, too scared, too tired to fight for what once felt like everything.

Now, I sit with the weight of what ifs pressing on my chest, wondering if we were a mistake or just a lesson wrapped in love.

And the worst part? I don't know which would hurt less.

"He gave me the worst punishment."
"What did he do? How dare he?" her friend snapped.

"He forgave me."

~broken soul

Wish I Could

I was not able to tell you.

Not when we spent hours talking about everything and
nothing.
Not when you memorized the way my voice changed with
my moods.
Not when you looked at me like I was the only person in
the world.
Not when you noticed the sadness in my texts, even when I
used all the right emojis to hide it.
Not when you made me feel understood in ways I didn't
even know I needed.

I was not able to tell you that there was someone else.
Someone I had already chosen.
Someone I was holding on to, even when they didn't hold
me the way you did.

And yet, I kept coming back to you-
for comfort, for laughter, for the warmth I wasn't supposed
to seek elsewhere.

You never asked for anything, never demanded a title,
never made me feel guilty-
but I saw the way you looked at me, the way you showed
up, the way you stayed.

You were always there, always listening, always giving-
while I took everything and gave nothing in return.

I knew what you felt.
I knew what I felt.
But I still stayed silent.

I let you wait for something I was never brave enough to
give.
And when you found out, the light in your eyes dimmed in
a way I can never forget.

You didn't get angry, you didn't ask why- you just left.
And that silence cut deeper than any words could.I was not
able to tell you the truth when it mattered.
I wish I could have told you, even once-

that I loved you too.

What We Left Behind

"Hey, look at this picture! Isn't this him? You guys dated, right?" her friend asked, holding up her phone.

She glanced at the screen, her expression unreadable. "Yeah... yeah, we did. It didn't work out, so we broke up. It's been almost four years now. The best thing is- it was mutual," she said, forcing a small smile.

"Oh, I see. Just saw his picture on some mutual friend's story," her friend shrugged. "Here, take a look."

She took the phone casually, but the moment her eyes landed on the screen, something shifted. Her fingers gripped the phone a little tighter.

Her friend noticed. "Is something wrong?"
Her voice came out quieter this time. "**His bracelet**..."
"What about it?"

She swallowed, feeling a strange tightness in her chest. "**That's my hairband**," she whispered.

And just like that, every moment, every memory came rushing back- the way he never asked for the breakup, how he had simply nodded and let her go, how he had smiled as if it didn't hurt, as if it was easy.

Had he ever truly wanted to let go? Or had he just wanted her to be happy- even if it meant losing her?

And now, she sits with the heaviest kind of regret- the one that comes from choosing to walk away from someone who was still holding on.

We Shouldn't Have Met

We shouldn't have met.
Not in that crowded room, not under that soft-lit sky.
Not when I was learning to love myself,
only to love you more instead.

We shouldn't have laughed the way we did,
turning quiet moments into memories
I can't seem to forget.

We shouldn't have talked for hours,
because now silence feels like punishment.
Like an empty space shaped exactly like you.

We shouldn't have made promises,
not when you knew you'd leave,
and I-
I was foolish enough to believe you wouldn't.

I shouldn't have let you in,
shouldn't have let you see the parts of me
no one else did.
Because now they belong to you,
even when you don't belong to me.

And maybe in another life,
we never meet.
And maybe that's the happiest ending
I'll never get to have.

---- ★ ----

THE REALIZATION

When truth settles in. Maybe it was love, maybe it wasn't. Maybe it was meant to stay, or maybe it was just meant to teach. Some things don't break you; they shape you.

You Already Have so Much

You think you're suffering just because someone left, because a love story didn't end the way you imagined.

But have you seen the mother who skips meals so her child doesn't sleep hungry? The father who works two jobs yet still worries if it's enough? The girl who lost her dream because society told her she couldn't? The boy who hides his tears because no one ever asked if he was okay?

There's a woman out there wishing for the freedom you take for granted. A man who would trade anything for the job you complain about.

Pain isn't a competition, but perspective is a gift. sometimes, stepping outside your own heartbreak makes you realize- there's so much more to life than the one who walked away.

Somewhere, someone is fighting battles you can't even imagine,someone is dreaming of the life you already have, yet they still wake up and try again. And maybe, just maybe, what you lost isn't as big as what you still have.

Just Because

Just because you love them deep,
Doesn't mean they own your sleep.

No one should steal your peace of mind,
No matter how their arms entwined.

If they cared, they wouldn't be,
The weight that drowns you endlessly.

Love should never feel like pain
Or leave you lost in endless rain

And one day, you'll come to see,
The ones who cared set your heart free.

Don't Afraid to Shine

You don't have to waste a single thought on people who believe , you only deserve flowers when you're dead.
You don't have to prove yourself to those who never believed in you to begin with.You don't have to seek love from hands that only hold you when it's convenient.

If something makes you happy, and it harms no one, do it. If something sets your soul on fire, chase it. If something feels right in your heart, trust it- no matter what they say, no matter who watches, no matter who whispers.

Because at the end of the day, the weight of their judgment will never be heavier than the weight of a life half-lived.

So don't forget to love, even when the world tries to make you doubt it. Don't forget to dream, even when they call it foolish. And don't forget to be you, unapologetically, loudly, boldly.

Because the right people won't ask you to shrink. They'll just remind you to shine.

Was Not Mine

I realize now-
love isn't supposed to feel like chasing,
like waiting for someone to care,
like proving you're worth the effort.

I realize now-
staying up overthought,
reading old texts like they held answers,
was never love, just my own illusion.

I realize now-
it wasn't fate,
wasn't some tragic love story,
just a lesson I refused to learn.

And in the end , I realize -
I was crying over something
that was never mine.

She Believed It

She stood in front of the mirror, her own reflection staring back at her- tired eyes, trembling hands, a face that had seen too much.

"Enough," it whispered. "Please, stop."

"You have cried enough for people who never looked back. You have broken yourself trying to fix others. You have questioned your worth because of someone who never deserved you."

"But have you forgotten?" the reflection asked.

"The nights you studied with swollen eyes while the world slept, just to build a future you once thought was impossible? The times you stood alone, holding yourself together when no one else did? The moments when life knocked you down, and yet, you got up every single time?"

"You were strong when you pushed through failure.

You were strong when you lost people you never imagined living without.
You were strong when you walked into rooms full of doubts and still proved yourself.
You were strong when the world told you 'you can't,' and you whispered back, 'watch me' ."

"You were strong then. You are strong now. And you will be strong tomorrow."

She wiped her tears, took a deep breath, and for the first time in a long time, she believed it.

85

Then Stop Complaining

You cursed the rain for ruining your day,
while a farmer looked at the sky, begging for just one drop.

You hated your job, the endless hours, the routine,
while someone wished for the luxury of a paycheck.

You frowned at your reflection, picking at flaws,
while someone else just wished they had a healthy body to
wake up in.

You complained about family, about expectations,
while someone sat alone, wishing they had a home to
return to.

And then one day, you saw it-
the pain, the longing, the silent prayers of others.
And once you realized that, none of it even mattered.
You stopped complaining.

Was It Really Love?

If you have to remind them to care, is it care?
If you have to fight for their time, is it even yours?
If you have to chase their attention, is it attention or just tolerance?
If you have to explain why you deserve effort, is it even respect?
If you have to question their intentions, was it ever real?
If their words say love but their actions don't, which one do you believe?
If you feel lonelier with them than without, is it love or just habit?

Love should feel like home, not like a test you keep failing.

Love isn't supposed to feel like a constant plea,
like convincing someone to stay,
like proving your worth over and over again.

Real love chooses you-
in the quiet moments, in the loud ones,
in the easy days and the hard ones.

If you have to beg, maybe it was never love .

You deserve better

Honestly, do you really think you deserve that? No, my friend.

You deserve people who lift you up, not those who tear you down with "just jokes." People who say, "I'm here for you," not those who use your insecurities as a punchline. You need the ones who make an effort to keep you, not the ones who take your presence for granted.

You deserve check-ins, not mixed signals. Reassurance, not silent treatments. Effort, not excuses. Love shouldn't feel like proving your worth, and friendship shouldn't feel like a test.

The right people won't make you beg for the bare minimum- they'll give it effortlessly.They won't make you question where you stand. They'll remind you- through their actions, not just their words- that you belong.

And when someone tells you, "You deserve better," it stings- until the day you realize you actually do.

So stop explaining yourself to people who refuse to understand. Stop holding onto those who make you feel like you're too much. You are not too much. You are enough. It's them who never had enough space to hold you.

They Were Never the Villain

Maybe they weren't the villain in your story. Maybe they never meant to hurt you. Maybe they were just a person trying to figure things out, just like you.

Not every heartbreak is a betrayal. Not every goodbye is a punishment. Sometimes, people leave not because they stopped caring, but because they didn't know how to stay. Maybe they were fighting battles they never spoke about. Maybe they were lost in ways you'll never understand.

It's easy to paint someone as the villain- it gives us closure, a reason to be angry. But the truth is, not everyone who leaves meant to break you. Some people simply weren't meant to stay.

And that's okay. It doesn't make them cruel, and it doesn't make you unworthy. It just means their chapter in your story has ended. And sometimes, the kindest thing you can do for yourself is to turn the page.

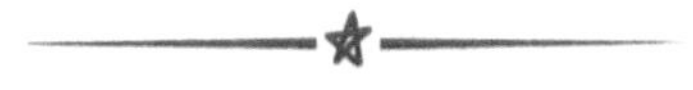

CHAPTER EIGHT

THE AWAKENING

The shift in perspective. Love exists beyond romance- It was always there, just in different forms.

How Much Is Too Much?

How much effort is too much effort?
No one tells you.
No one warns you when love turns into sacrifice,
when giving becomes losing,
when staying starts to feel like sinking.

You bend, you break, you bleed-
but they only notice when you stop.
You whisper your needs,
but they only listen when you leave.

And that's okay.
Because now, you know.
Love shouldn't feel like convincing.
Respect shouldn't feel like a reward.
Effort shouldn't feel like exhaustion.

You were never asking for too much.
You were just asking the wrong ones.

Was It Love or Just the Attention?

Was it love, or just the habit of having someone to text at night?
Was it care, or just the comfort of knowing someone was there?
Was it special, or just the way they made you feel wanted for a while?
Did you love them, or did you love how they made you feel?
Did you love them, or just the feeling of being wanted?
Did you miss them, or just the version of yourself when they were around?

Sometimes, it's not love we lose-
it's the attention, the comfort, the routine.

And that hurts too.so be clear abou it first .

I lost you and thought I was gone,
But in the silence,

I found my own song

That hit me Hard

It hits hard when bruh says, "You can't be the good person in everyone's story."

Because no matter how much kindness you pour, how much effort you give, or how deeply you love- there will always be someone who sees it differently. Not every action will be understood the way you intended. Not every apology will be enough. Not every sacrifice will be noticed. And sometimes, no matter how much you try, you will still be the villain in someone's story.

But that doesn't mean you weren't good. It doesn't mean you didn't deserve better. It just means people choose to see what they want to see. They hold on to your mistakes, not your efforts. They remember the times you fell short, not the countless times you showed up. That's the rule of the world- people pick faults before they acknowledge greatness. Just like they can't find a reason to blame the rose, so instead, they call it thorned.

And that... that hit me hard.

Help Them Go

I held on like the ocean hugs the shore,
even as the waves pulled me away.

I tried, I stayed, I fought so hard,
but love can't live in a one-sided heart.

I fought for us with trembling hands,
but love is not a battle meant for one.

So I stepped back, I let you go,
watched the tide take you slow.

Because if someone is trying to lose you,
don't hold on- help them go.

Love Exists

When I thought love didn't exist,

I saw my father cooking while my mother lay sick.
I saw my mother standing by him, even when she had no idea what he was doing.
I saw my sister slipping money into my wallet when she thought I wasn't looking.
I saw a brother walking on the roadside so I wouldn't have to.
I saw a grandmother keeping candies for a grandchild who rarely visited.
I saw a friend staying up late, just to hear me rant about my bad day.
I saw a teacher who never gave up on the quiet kid in the back.
I saw a stranger holding the door a little longer, just so no one felt left behind.
I saw a colleague covering my shift when they knew I needed a break.
I saw a neighbor leaving food at my doorstep when I was too sick to cook.
I saw a taxi driver turning down the meter because he knew I was short on cash.
I saw a passerby stopping to tie a child's undone shoelace.
I saw an old couple holding hands like they were still living their first love story.
I saw a little kid sharing their last piece of candy without a second thought.
I saw a shopkeeper rounding off the bill just to make things easier for a struggling customer.

I saw a dog waiting by the door, tail wagging, proving that love never asks for anything in return.
I saw a stranger picking up someone's fallen groceries like it was the most natural thing to do.
I saw love in places where no words were spoken, only actions.

Love exists. In gestures too small for the world to notice but big enough to mean everything.

His Awakening

At first, he thought love was something he had to earn-through effort, through sacrifice, through bending himself into shapes that no longer felt like home. He believed if he gave enough, stayed long enough, proved himself enough, they would choose him.

But then, it hit him- love was never meant to be a test.

He saw the truth, not in a grand moment, but in the quiet way his heart grew tired. He realized his worth was not tied to who stayed or who left. It was never about being more for someone else- it was about being enough for himself.

And so, he stopped chasing. Stopped proving. Stopped begging for love that needed convincing.

Because real love- the kind that lasts- doesn't ask you to shrink. It meets you where you stand.

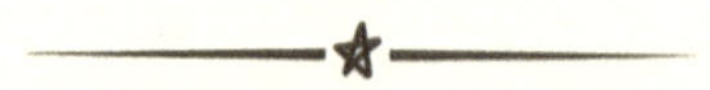

The Healing

*When the weight lightens. When the past loses its grip,
wounds turn into wisdom. When you learn to carry love
without pain, without expectation.*

More Than Enough

There was a time when I gave my love freely- to those who needed it the most. I held their hands when they were lost, gave them warmth when the world turned cold. I listened to stories no one else had the patience for. I made space for them in my life without asking for a place in theirs.

And for the longest time, I thought love meant giving without expecting, that kindness wasn't meant to be returned. But then I found myself standing alone, wondering why I felt so empty when all I ever did was pour.

Should I regret it? Should I wish I had kept more for myself?

No.
Because I was there when they had no one. I was the home they ran to, the light they borrowed when theirs had burned out.

Maybe they left, maybe they forgot. But I was what they needed when they needed it.
And that is enough.
That is more than enough.

The Moment You Accept

You don't have to forget to move on,
you don't have to be unbroken to heal.

Some days, the past will whisper,
some nights, the ache will return.
But you are not where you were,
and that is enough.

Slowly, the weight will lighten,
the wounds will turn into lessons,
the love you lost will make space
for the love you deserve.

And one day, you'll realize-
the moment you accept your pain,
healing starts.

She Found Herself

She started reading again- not to escape, but because she finally wanted to.
She played her favorite songs, not to drown out the silence, but because the silence no longer hurt.
She laughed- not the forced kind, not the kind that hid the cracks, but the kind that felt real, full, alive.

It's not that she's distracting herself anymore. She's not pretending to be okay.
She just is.

She doesn't flinch when she hears his name. She doesn't reread old messages, looking for answers that will never come. She doesn't wonder if he ever thinks of her.

Because she has finally realized- she doesn't need him to.

Healing didn't happen all at once. It was slow, messy, and full of nights where she swore she'd never get here. But she did. Not because time healed her, not because someone new saved her, but because she saved herself.

She is strong enough to let go.
Strong enough to move forward.

Strong enough to know that she was always whole- she just had to remember it.

The Softness of Moving On

At first, you think healing means proving something- to them, to yourself, to the world. You go out more, you post happier pictures, you fill the silence with distractions, convincing yourself you're okay.

Maybe you even try to replace them with someone new, hoping that if someone else holds your hand, their absence won't sting as much. But deep down, you know- using one person to forget another never works. Attachment isn't a switch you can flip. Love isn't a joke you can rewrite with a different name.

But then, something shifts. One day, you hear their name, and your heart doesn't drop. You see a picture of them, and instead of pain, all you feel is... nothing. Not bitterness, not regret- just peace. That's when you realize: moving on was never about getting even, never about pretending it didn't hurt. It was about accepting what was, forgiving what couldn't be, and freeing yourself from the weight of what-ifs.

You don't wish them pain. You don't wish them back. You simply wish them well- and for the first time, you mean it.

"Healing isn't about proving you've moved on. It's when you no longer need to."

The Quiet Arrival

I stopped searching for them in strangers,
stopped rewriting the past in my head.
Their memory became a story I once lived,
not a place where I still bled.

It wasn't sudden- it was slow,
like winter melting into spring.
One morning, I woke up and realized-
I no longer ached for what was missing.

I Don't Hate You

Loving you was never the mistake. I never regretted the way my heart softened at your touch, the way I gave you all the love I had, without hesitation, without fear. I don't regret the way I showed up for you, even on the days when you barely noticed. I don't regret the patience, the kindness, the unwavering belief that maybe- just maybe- you would learn how to love me the same way.

But I do regret thinking you knew what to do with that love. I regret believing you would hold it gently instead of letting it slip through your fingers like it meant nothing. I regret assuming you understood its weight, its depth, its rarity. Because love like mine wasn't common, and maybe that's why you didn't know how to keep it.

Still, I don't hate you. I don't wish I never met you. Because love is never wasted. What you give out always finds its way back to you. That's the rule of the universe- what you send into the world, you receive in return. Maybe not from the same person, maybe not in the way you expected, but it always comes back.

So, no.... I don't regret loving you. Because one day, that same love will return to me, in a heart that's ready to hold it. And when it does, I'll finally understand why you had to let it go.

Healing is Not Avoiding

Attraction is not love,
and love is not possession.
Silence is not peace,
and healing is not suppression.

Forgetting is not moving on,
and moving on is not erasing.
Scars don't mean weakness,
and pain is not a life sentence.

Healing is standing where it broke you
and feeling nothing but peace.
It's looking at the past
without wishing it had been different.

It's not pretending it never hurt-
it's knowing it no longer does.

Healed more Than You realize

You've healed more than you realize. Let me tell you how.

You stop checking their online status. Not because you don't care, but because you no longer seek answers in their silence.

You hear an old song, the one that once made you break down, and now? It's just a song. The memories don't sting the way they used to.

You no longer over-explain yourself to people who have already made up their minds about you. You let them misunderstand. You let them go.

You stop chasing people who make you question your worth. Instead, you gravitate toward those who make you feel at home, without trying too hard.

You smile when you see kids playing, not because it's just a cute sight, but because their laughter reminds you of a joy that still exists within you.

You feel sadness for a stranger's pain, not because you know them, but because your heart is soft enough to understand that suffering has no boundaries.

You celebrate others' wins without envy, because you've learned that someone else's success doesn't take away from your own.

You no longer blame your parents for what they couldn't give you, because you've realized they did the best they could with what they had.

You don't seek revenge, closure, or explanations from those who hurt you- you just move forward, knowing peace is worth more than proving a point.

You see a couple holding hands, and instead of feeling

bitter, you smile. Love doesn't feel like a threat anymore. It feels like something you'll welcome when the time is right. You scroll past success stories without comparing timelines. You know that your journey is yours alone, and what's meant for you will never miss you.

You no longer hold grudges- not because they deserve forgiveness, but because you deserve peace.

You look in the mirror, and instead of picking apart your flaws, you whisper, "I'm doing okay." And for the first time in a long time, you actually mean it.

And most importantly, you've stopped waiting for happiness to arrive someday. You've started finding it in the small things, the quiet moments, the everyday miracles you once overlooked.

That's healing. That's growth. That's you- becoming whole again.

Becoming Your Own Home

You no longer wait for someone to come and fix you- you've learned to hold yourself together. You've stopped searching for love in places that never kept you warm.

You don't chase closure anymore, because you've realized it's not something they can give you- it's something you give yourself.

Somewhere along the way, you stopped asking, "Why did this happen to me?" and started saying, "Maybe this happened for me."

Healing isn't about pretending it never hurt. It's about knowing you don't have to hurt forever. It's about realizing that peace isn't in moving on fast- it's in moving on fully.

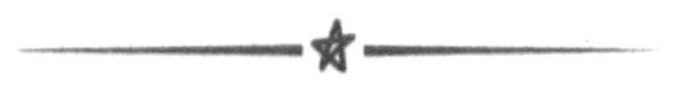

CHAPTER TEN

THE PEACE

The quiet understanding. Accepting what was, appreciating what is, and embracing what's to come- with softness, not sorrow.

Peace ???

There was a time
when their name felt like a wound,
when memories clung like shadows,
when silence was the loudest sound.

But days turned into months,
and the weight became lighter.
The echoes faded,
the pain softened,
the love remained-
not as longing,
but as something gentle,
something I no longer needed to hold.

Peace wasn't forgetting,
it was learning to remember
without breaking.

The Peace That Came Quietly

The evening sky burned in shades of orange and lilac as he sat on his balcony, the city humming in the background. A gentle breeze played with his hair, carrying whispers of a past that no longer hurt.

He thought of the people who once felt like forever, the moments that once defined him. The laughter, the late-night conversations, the goodbyes that shattered him- all of it still lived in him, but not as wounds. Not anymore.

He used to wonder why things fell apart, why some people left when he was still holding on. But now, he just smiled at the memories. After all, he had loved them once- how could he ever hate them?

Maybe he never got the answers he searched for, but somewhere along the way, he stopped needing them. He healed without realizing it. Life moved forward, and so did he.

Because God's plan was always better. And even if he couldn't see it then, he could feel it now- in the quiet, in the calm, in the way his heart no longer ached for what was never meant to stay.

Avenge Is Not Your Thing

You do not seek revenge,
not because you couldn't,
but because you know it wouldn't change a thing.

You do not wish them pain,
not because they didn't deserve it,
but because you deserve peace more than they deserve
punishment.

You do not look back with anger,
not because it didn't hurt,
but because you refuse to let the past hold you prisoner.

Your healing is not in proving a point,
not in making them regret,
not in watching them suffer-
it is in waking up one day
and realizing they no longer have power over you.

Avenge was never your thing.
Peace always was.

The Weight of Peace

She finally realized- it was never a mistake, only a lesson. A chapter written not to break her, but to build her. Every tear, every heartbreak, every unanswered question wasn't a punishment; it was preparation.

God wasn't being cruel. He was teaching her strength, patience, and the art of letting go. He was showing her that some people come as blessings, and others as lessons, but none were ever meant to stay forever.

She no longer resents the past. She no longer aches for what was or questions what could have been. She sees it now for what it is- just a story she once lived, not a home she has to stay in.

And that is peace. Not forgetting, not erasing, but accepting.

Smiling at the past, embracing the present, and trusting that whatever is meant for her will never have to be chased.

The Closure You Give Yourself

You thought healing meant hearing the words I'm sorry-but it never came, and somehow, you survived. It wasn't their regret that set you free. It was the moment you stopped waiting for it.

One day, the past stopped feeling like an open wound. The memories didn't change, but their weight did. The names, the voices, the nights spent overthinking- it all softened, faded, lost its power.

You don't hate them. You don't miss them. You don't even wish things had been different. You just accept-and in that acceptance, you find the peace you were searching for all along.

Because closure was never about what they could give you. It was about what you finally gave yourself.

The Power of Letting Go

Life turns peaceful when you stop arguing to be understood.It becomes beautiful when you no longer seek closure.

Not every truth needs to be spoken, not every wound needs to be avenged.Some things heal in silence, some goodbyes are the answer themselves.

You don't need the last word to find peace.
You don't need an apology to move on.
You don't need them to understand- you just need to let go.

Because real freedom isn't in proving your worth,

it's in realizing you were enough all along-
that the right people never needed convincing,
and the wrong ones were never worth the fight.

Let Love Find You

The more you search for love, the more you stumble upon the wrong people- the ones who feel right for a moment but leave you questioning everything in the end.

Love isn't something you chase. It's something that finds you when you're ready, when you're whole, when you no longer need it to complete you.

So don't fear love just because it once hurt you. Don't hesitate to fall again. Love is not the enemy-
choosing the wrong hands to hold it was. The right love won't demand proof of your worth. It won't leave you exhausted from trying. It will come gently, unexpectedly, and stay effortlessly.

Until then, focus on yourself. Heal. Grow. And trust- what's meant for you will always find its way.

Loving, Losing and Becoming

Loving was easy- until it wasn't. Until love demanded more than just feelings, until it tested patience, trust, and the strength to stay.

Losing felt unbearable- until it became necessary. Until it taught that some things are meant to be felt, not kept. That no matter how tightly you hold on, what isn't yours will always find a way to leave.

Becoming was the hardest- until it became freeing. Until the pain turned into wisdom, the heartbreak into growth, and the past into a story, not a prison.

This journey wasn't about winning or losing. It was about transformation. About learning that love is not possession, loss is not the end, and becoming is the only way forward.

And now, here you are- not just surviving, but evolving. Not just moving on, but rising. Stronger. Wiser. Whole.

No matter how heavy your heart feels right now, no matter how unfair life seems- one day, you'll look back and understand why it all happened the way it did.

The nights you cried yourself to sleep, the moments you questioned your worth, the times you begged for things to stay- every single piece of your pain was shaping you into who you were meant to become.

Life is never just about what you lose. It's about what you find in yourself when you think you have nothing left.

Trust the process. Trust your growth. Trust that every heartbreak, every unanswered prayer, every ending was just another step toward something better.

And one day, you won't be angry anymore. You won't be asking "Why me?" You'll simply smile and say, Now I see why.

And One Day, It All Makes Sense .

THE END

Until We Meet Again In Words

Dear Reader,

Thank you for giving your precious time to this book. It means more than words can express. Every page, every word was written with heart, and knowing that you chose to read it is a gift in itself.

I hope these pieces spoke to you, made you feel seen, or simply kept you company for a little while. If even a single line stayed with you, then this journey was worth it.

With all my gratitude and warmth,
Paresh Singh Rajput :)